© Aladdin Books Ltd 1990

Design   David West
                      Children's Book Design
Editor   Steve Parker
Photo researcher   Cecilia Weston-Baker
Consultant   Dr. Michael Gossop

First published in the   The publishers would like to
United States in 1990 by   acknowledge that the photographs
Franklin Watts   reproduced within this book have
387 Park Avenue South   been posed by models or have
New York NY 10016   been obtained from photographic
                                agencies
Printed in Belgium

Library of Congress Cataloging-in-Publication Data
Condon, Judith.
    The pressure to take drugs/Judith Condon.
      p. cm. -- (Understanding drugs)
      Summary: Discusses how many young people become involved with c
    taking due to peer pressure, and gives advice to resist and avoid
    drugs.
      ISBN 0-531-10934-8
      1. Children--Drug use--Juvenile literature. 2. Children--Drug
    use--Prevention--Juvenile literature. 3. Peer pressure--Juvenile
    literature. [1. Drug abuse.] I. Title. II. Series.
    HV5824.C45C66   1990
    362.29'12'083--dc20   89-70581   CIP   AC

Contents

UNDERSTANDING DRUGS

THE PRESSURE TO TAKE DRUGS

Judith Condon

FRANKLIN WATTS
London · New York · Toronto · Sydney

INTRODUCTION

Hardly a day goes by without news headlines on the worldwide evils of drug abuse. Usually the drug in question will be heroin, cocaine or crack. These are the drugs people kill for; the drugs which poor farmers grow, rich dealers sell, and governments seem unable to stamp out.

But this is not the whole story. The most widely abused drugs in western society are tobacco and alcohol, which over the years have ruined millions of people's lives and the health of whole nations. Moreover, some countries fail to control the abuse of medical drugs, including tranquilizers, and they do not control the drugs used in livestock farming.

The pressures to take drugs apply to any drug. No one fully understands why some people respond to pressure in one way, some in another. Each of us has a unique genetic makeup and a particular life history. We tend to think we know ourselves better the older we get. But sometimes life can surprise us.

Take, for example, the person at work who always appears confident and good humored. It may be that this person is very sensitive underneath, and depends on an orderly and secure lifestyle. If suddenly made redundant or caught up in a crisis, this apparently calm person may "go to pieces," perhaps starting on the road to self-destructive behavior such as alcoholism.

At times everyone suffers stress or anxiety.

Some people think that being young is to be carefree, and not suffer stress. It's not true. Young people can feel anxious, bored, frustrated, afraid, guilty and ambitious, just like older people – and probably more so. Changing from a child into an adult, taking exams, learning to get along with people, not having much money – there are many things to cope with. You can't assume that it will never happen to you. You cannot predict how you will respond to all the pressures life can pile on top of you.

This book is written in the belief that knowledge is power, especially when you are under pressure. The more you learn about why people take drugs, and what the dangers are, the better equipped you should be to make the right choices and safeguard your own health. The more we know as a society, the higher our chances of cutting down the pressure and finding an alternative way.

> **People always said how sensible I was as a youngster. They never guessed I would end up like this. Neither did I. Publishing consultant.**

6

What is a drug?

The word "drug" is used to cover a wide range of sub-stances, both natural and synthetic. This means that the use of the word "drug" can be very confusing. It is important to know what the most common drugs are, and how they work, before thinking about why people use them.

A drug is a substance that affects the body or the mind, or both, in certain ways. Because some drugs affect the mind, they have effects on a person's behavior.

Medicinal drugs

First, there are the medicinal drugs – those used to treat sickness or to keep people healthy or to help them live longer. Sometimes they are used for a limited time. For example, a course of antibiotics can help to cure or prevent bacterial infection and fight against certain kinds of virus. Short-term use of painkillers can enable patients to be comfortable after surgery, until they heal.

Other medical drugs may be used over a longer time, to assist chronic (long-term) complaints. They may aid the pumping of a diseased heart, or control diabetes, or help to lower blood pressure. The discovery of such drugs has been of great benefit to humankind. But medical drugs must be taken only for specific purposes and on medical advice. Even so, great care has to be taken over their correct use and they can have unwanted side effects.

Everyday drugs: caffeine

The second group of drugs are what might be called

"everyday drugs," or "social drugs." Perhaps the most widespread is caffeine, the stimulant substance found in coffee, tea, chocolate, and some soft drinks. People who drink coffee at regular times of the day, when they need a "lift" or a "pick-me-up," may not realize that they are consuming a drug.

> *I used to drink a lot of coffee, but I could never get to sleep at night. The doctor told me to keep a record of how much I drank. One day I counted 20 cups. I cut down to three cups a day. Now I'm fine.* **Young woman office worker.** 99

Alcohol, cigarettes, chocolate and painkillers all contain forms of "everyday drugs."

But if you drink several cups of strong coffee in a day, it can leave you tense and can cause acid indigestion.

Everyday drugs: alcohol

In many parts of the world, alcohol is widely used in the form of beers, wines, ciders and spirits. Indeed, the drinking of alcohol is very much part of our culture. Many people find it impossible to imagine a social gathering – whether it's a birthday party, a wedding, or even a funeral – where alcohol is not consumed. Most people find alcohol pleasantly relaxing when taken occasionally and in moderate amounts. But people who drink too much can cause harm to themselves and to others.

Alcohol holds dangers for young people especially.

The effects of alcohol on young people can be particularly severe, and because of bodily differences, its effects are stronger on women than on men. Misuse of alcohol, even on a single occasion, can cause not only a severe hangover, but also death. Around one half of all car drivers and two thirds of pedestrians killed in road accidents have been found to have high levels of alcohol in their blood.

In the longer term, alcohol abuse can lead to cirrhosis of the liver and alcoholism. Heavy drinkers often have trouble holding down a job. This drug sometimes encourages violent or abusive behavior, leading to trouble with the law and the breakup of relationships and families.

Everyday drugs: nicotine

The third "everyday" drug is nicotine, a substance found in the tobacco plant, and known to be addictive. When someone smokes a cigarette and inhales the smoke, it takes only a few seconds for the nicotine in the smoke to pass from the lungs into the blood, and then to the brain. This drug makes the smoker feel temporarily more relaxed or more alert. Tobacco smoke is also breathed in by other people nearby, turning them into "passive smokers."

During this century, the smoking habit has spread throughout the world. It causes illness and premature death on a massive scale. The main diseases linked to smoking are heart conditions, lung cancer, and other lung conditions such as emphysema and bronchitis. The problem is so great that smoking has been called one of the major health issues of our time.

Snorting cocaine gives a brief "high" – and a long-term problem

Illegal drugs

In your mind, you may have an image of people who use illegal drugs. Perhaps you see a down-and-out addict injecting heroin, or a group of punk-style youths sniffing glue. Most people have stereotyped ideas about illegal drugs. The truth is that these drugs exist in many different forms, and under a confusing number of names, and it is not so simple to say who uses them and why.

Heroin

Perhaps the most widely feared drug is heroin, made from the opium poppy. Heroin is a painkiller, and highly addictive. When someone takes heroin, his or her brain reacts quickly by changing the way the body's natural painkillers (endorphins) work. If heroin is later withheld, the body's natural painkillers cannot cope. The result is severe withdrawal symptoms, like a bad case of influenza.

Regular heroin users become tolerant of the drug; that is, they need bigger and bigger amounts to get the same effect. Soon their whole life starts to revolve around getting a supply of the drug.

Cocaine and other stimulants

Cocaine has its effects by stimulating the nervous system. Someone who "snorts" cocaine gets a very fast and very short-lived "high." Similarly amphetamines, often called "uppers" or "speed," have the power to speed up the whole body, lifting the person's mood, and delaying sleep. High doses of both drugs can cause extreme nervousness and anxiety. As with heroin, the body tries to counteract the drug. When the effect of the drug passes, the person is left feeling tired and weakened.

❝❝ *Official tests at a horse race revealed that the winning horse had traces of drugs in its blood. Then the stable girl confessed. She'd fed it a chocolate bar before the race. The horse was disqualified.* **News report.** ❞❞

Hallucinogens

Another group of drugs, the hallucinogens, works in a different way. They alter how the brain interprets the signals

Glue sniffing causes drowsiness and can lead to unconsciousness.

it receives from the senses. People feel that they see colors more brightly, or that they hear sounds in an unfamiliar way. Hallucinogens are drugs that cause false perception or mental illusions. The most widely used of these is marijuana, also known as *cannabis sativa*. It can make people feel pleasantly relaxed and talkative, but it can also affect the memory and concentration, causing problems if the person is driving or operating machinery. "Magic mushrooms" have a stronger but similar effect.

Most powerful in the hallucinogen group are LSD ("acid") and PCP ("angel dust"), which are laboratory-made. When swallowed they produce hallucinations, feelings of strange insight and distortion, and sometimes a sense of panic. Individuals "high" on LSD have been killed by, for example, believing that they could fly from high buildings, or stop a speeding car by stepping in front of it, or cut themselves and not bleed.

Inhalants

A fourth group of drugs includes solvents and gases found in household products. When inhaled through the nose or mouth, they have the power to depress, or damp down, the nervous system. The person loses self-control, begins to feel drowsy or giddy, and may lapse into unconsciousness.

Many of the deaths that have occurred among young people sniffing glue or similar substances result from suffocation or from inhaling their own vomit.

In many countries, it is not illegal to possess substances that could be abused as inhalants. Indeed, many of them are useful products around the house and in the workshop. In most circumstances, the emphasis is on store owners and retail staff. They must judge whether people (usually young people) are buying the product for its intended purpose, or to misuse it by inhaling the fumes. Often, store signs say that glues and similar solvent products will not be sold to people under a certain age.

Society's attitude toward drugs

Clearly it is not possible to talk about drugs as if they were all the same. Some are legal, some are not; some cure, some kill; some slow the body down, some speed it up.

Society struggles to take account of these differences, but does not always succeed. Sometimes it is for historical

Young people face strong pressure to take up smoking.

reasons that one drug is deemed acceptable, at least in moderation, while another drug may be banned – even though it is less harmful – simply because it arrived later on the scene.

Then again, different societies take different views. In Britain, for example, there is a serious problem of alcohol abuse among teenagers, who are allowed to buy alcohol at 18 years of age, but who often start drinking younger than that. In the United States you have to be 21 before you can buy alcohol. Yet American teenagers are more likely to use marijuana and cocaine. No society has all the answers. And outlawing a substance does not always prevent people from using it.

LEGAL DRUGS			ILLEGAL DRUGS	
Type	Found in	Effect	Type	Method of Taking
Caffeine	Coffee, tea, chocolate, soft drinks	Mild stimulation	Heroin, "junk," "scag," "smack"	Smoked, sniffed, injected
Alcohol	Wine, beer, cider, spirits	Relaxation by depressing the nervous system	Cocaine, "coke," "snow," "freebase"	Sniffed up nose ("snorted")
Nicotine	Cigarettes, pipe tobacco, chewing tobacco	Relaxes and stimulates	Crack, "rock"	Smoked
Medicinal drugs and medicines	Prescribed by doctor	Fight disease regulate the body's workings	Amphetamines, "speed," "uppers"	Swallowed as pills, sniffed or smoked
Benzo-diazepines	Tranquilizers	Relieve worry and anxiety	Marijuana, "pot," "dope," "grass"	Smoked on its own or with tobacco
Barbiturates	Sleeping pills	Promote sleep	LSD, "acid," "angel dust"	Swallowed as pills or drops on blotting paper
Drugs for minor ailments	Cough mixtures, aspirins paracetamol	Ease pain and help healing	Solvents and gases, glues, aerosols	Inhaled through nose and/or mouth

Who needs protecting?

Young people may come to the conclusion that society's attitude toward drugs is unfair or hypocritical. They may feel that they cannot trust well-meaning but not well-informed adults, who speak in general terms about "drugs" without knowing much about specific drugs and the specific problems they create. What should a child make of the parent who warns, "If I ever see you with drugs you'll be out of this house!" – when the same parent smokes 40 cigarettes a day and gets roaring drunk every Saturday night?

Society has a duty to try and protect young people from being exploited by legal drug manufacturers, and from

17

Medicinal drugs should only be taken on doctors' prescription.

coming to harm at the hands of those who manufacture and sell illegal drugs. At the same time, most young people want to make up their own minds. The most important thing is to know the facts about drugs. That way, you will know the drawbacks and the dangers. Only then can you start to make the right choices for yourself.

> **In its 24-week life a pig for market is fed a steady diet of "growth boosting" hormones, which speed up weight gain. Residues of the drugs turn up in the pork we eat. News report.**

MEDICINAL DRUGS

" Thousands of drugs are made under different brand names... "

A pill for everything?

Millions of lives have been saved during this century by the development of modern drugs. Thanks to such drugs, diseases like polio and tuberculosis no longer hold the terror that they used to. As a result, people put much more faith in pills and medicines. Some people feel let down if they leave the doctor's room without a prescription. They have come to believe that there must be a pill for everything.

The lesson of tranquilizers

You can see how this pressure works if you look at what happened with tranquilizer drugs.

In the past, people who ran into problems with their lives might have gone for advice to a priest or an older member of the family. When they looked to their doctor for help, they complained of depression, tiredness or "nerves." Doctors really had nothing to offer such patients except a sympathetic ear. They could not write a prescription for a new job, or a better place to live, or a more loving family.

At the start of the 1960s, drugs of a new type became available: the "minor tranquilizers." They were marketed under brand names such as Valium and Librium, and they promised to be able to change a person's mood. The drugs seemed to suit everyone, especially some doctors. Not only did they now have pills to offer people suffering from stress or anxiety, but the pills were quite cheap. And it took very little time to write a prescription.

Aspirin relieve pain but should not be taken on a regular bas

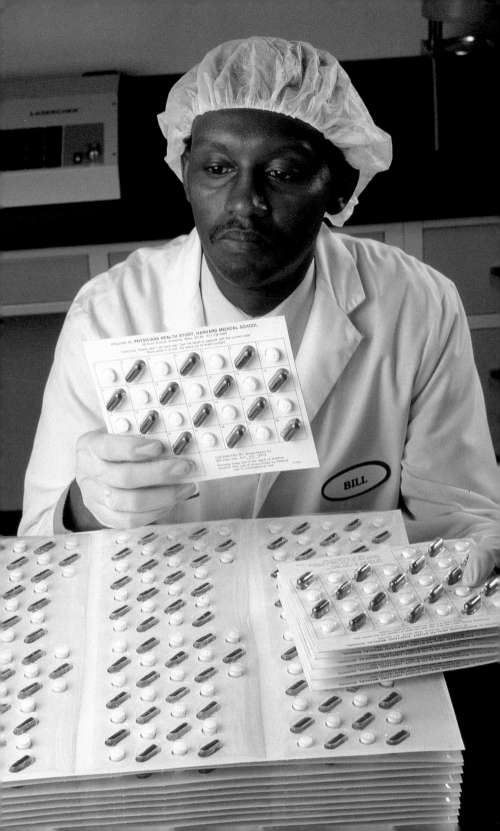

Tranquilizers were originally meant to be "short term" drugs, designed to be taken for one or a few weeks, to help people get over a crisis in their lives. Instead, they were sometimes given for months or years on end. They were advised for women suffering from isolation, bringing up children by themselves. They were given to young people upset after the break-up of a love relationship. They were even given out routinely to residents of old people's homes to make them more docile and easier for the staff and relatives to deal with.

Many people received repeat prescriptions for years, without ever being seen by a doctor. After a while, they found that they were addicted. And not only that, they also found that they had lost the ability to think clearly. Their minds were in a constant "fog." This discovery caused a scandal in the medical community.

People want doctors they can talk to and trust. They want guidance, support, kindness, and caring. But they get drugs. Dr Vernon Coleman, in *The Health Scandal: Your Health in Crisis.*

Today, doctors are more aware of the problems which tranquilizers cause. They may be useful for short term treatment – for example, when someone has been bereaved and needs help getting through the first few days of shock. But they do not provide easy long-term solutions. Indeed, because they suppress a person's feelings, they can make the real problems harder to recognize. Sooner or later that bereaved person will need love and support, and will need help to release the grief without drugs.

The wrong expectations

Our society has gotten into the habit of taking pills and medicines.

One estimate suggests that one half of the adult population and one third of all children take some form of medication every day. Much of it is totally unnecessary and a waste of resources.

The person who overeats and then goes to the doctor for diet pills, or the person who smokes and goes to the doctor for cough medicine, does not really need medication at all. A change of eating habits, or giving up smoking, is the only real solution. There is no easy short cut. Drugs are a temporary and artificial measure.

Even in the case of serious diseases such as polio and tuberculosis, drugs did not provide all the answers. Social measures were more important. Advances such as better housing, proper sewage disposal, clean drinking water, and adequate supplies of good food, laid the foundations of public health. The drugs were only one factor in conquering these illnesses.

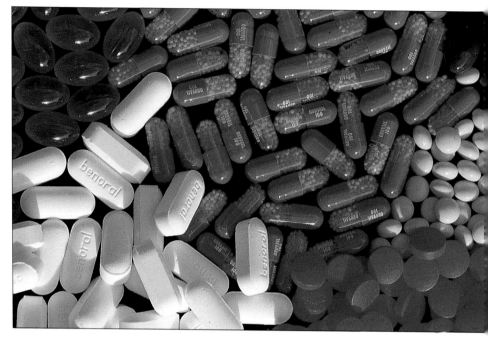

Drug companies spend huge sums to market their products.

Drug companies

Patients put doctors under pressure. So, too, do the companies that manufacture drugs. These companies are important to us all. They carry out research, and they develop new products. For example, at present many scientists are striving to find an effective treatment for AIDS other than zidovudine or AZT.

However, they are also in business to make money. Obviously they want people to put faith in their products, so that they can sell lots of them. Many of these products are useful, but some are not. Every year the drug companies spend millions of dollars worldwide on advertising and promotion. They pay for adverts in medical journals, send doctors free gifts, and pay for them to go to conferences in exotic places. They also influence the medical profession by funding colleges and professional organizations.

❝❝ *The World Health Organization's list of essential drugs for 1985 ran to only 200 products. Yet thousands of drugs are made under different brand names. Every year the drug companies spend millions of dollars persuading doctors to use their products. Many ads are for the same drug, under different names.* UK Consumer Organisation ❞❞

The same kind of pressure is felt by veterinary surgeons and farmers. They are urged to use hormone drugs to increase the milk yield in cattle, or to increase the size of their pigs. Some of these drugs remain in the meat or milk. They may cause harm to the human consumer. This is a new procedure and food scientists have not yet been able to do long-term studies and surveys.

In some parts of the world, where medical advice is hard to come by and very expensive, people are even encouraged to buy drugs such as antibiotics over the counter, at their local store. Yet they may not take the right antibiotic, and they may not take the right dose. One serious result of using antibiotics too freely is that germs adapt and become resistant to them. In time, a new breed of germs develops and existing antibiotics have no effect on them.

This kind of commercial pressure has helped create a society in which people turn too easily to drugs.

New ways of looking at health

If many of the diseases of "nature" have now been wiped out, why are we all not super-fit? What has happened is that the old diseases have been replaced by new ones: the diseases of "civilization." In modern industrial societies we get ill mainly because of how we live. We eat too much fatty food, we abuse our bodies with tobacco and alcohol, and we get too little exercise. Ill health can also be caused as a side effect of medical drug treatments. In addition, we suffer the effects of bad living or working conditions, industrial pollution, and stress.

Many people today prefer not to rely so much on pills. They try to take responsibility for their own health, and for the environment in which they live and work. They believe this is the best way to avoid ill health and live life to the fullest.

❝❝ *Many people, especially the elderly, have bathroom cabinets full of unused medicinal drugs. Many of these drugs are past their expiration dates, and could be dangerous.* **News report.** ❞❞

Social pressure

When you are young, the pressure to take up smoking and drinking can be strong. But much depends on the people around you. Some families avoid tobacco and alcohol for religious reasons. This does not mean their children are immune, but if they do not see other people smoking and drinking regularly, they are less likely to think of it themselves. On the other hand, hearing a smoker cough every morning, or seeing your parents acting aggressively when drunk, can put you off for life. So can seeing how much money they waste.

Small children learn by copying. For example, if their parents smoke, they often imitate the actions of smoking.

For some children, cigarettes are part of everyday life.

They think of it as something adults do. Teenagers do the same. They think that by adopting adult habits they will seem grown up themselves. Yet, smoking is not a natural part of adult life. Only one adult in three smokes. And most adults do not drink alcohol to excess.

Some teenagers start using cigarettes or alcohol when under pressure of exams, for example, or if they are bored, or to try and give them confidence when out on a date. In one way, it is natural to want to try things out for yourself. You may even think of it as an act of rebellion.

The problem is that things can get out of control. You can get addicted to smoking before you realize it. And how will you know when you have had too much to drink? Far from looking grown up or cool, you can soon become stupidly drunk, embarrassing both yourself and your friends! Some young people think that being drunk is acceptable behavior, but it involves the risk of alcoholism. You may also get into trouble with the law or other authority if you are aggressive when you get drunk.

❝ *The pressure to smoke cigarettes is strongest when you're a teenager. Hardly anyone starts smoking as an adult.* **Anti-smoking poster.** **❞**

Pressure from advertising

Advertisements for cigarettes and alcohol do influence young people, even though many countries put restrictions on what the advertisers are allowed to say. Cigarette companies aim their ads at particular groups. In recent years they have targeted young women, who have become more independent and have more money to spend.

In countries where tobacco firms can advertise freely, adverts still make out smoking to be sexy or glamorous. Needless to say, they never mention heart disease, lung cancer, or even the smell of stale cigarette butts. In the same way, ads for alcohol make drinking seem cool and sophisticated. They never contain pictures of poor people or people who have drunk too much and been involved in car accidents or fights.

Sponsorship

When countries such as Britain and the United States cut down on cigarette advertising, the tobacco companies tried a new tactic. They began sponsoring sports and the arts. By paying money to televised sports such as football, car racing, golf, tennis, and cricket, they kept their brand names in the public eye. Young people especially watch a lot of sports at events and on television.

Sport is about being fit and healthy. Smoking is just the opposite, and most sports people do not smoke. Sponsorship is a form of cheating. It is a form of advertising through the back door.

Drinks such as beer and ale are also promoted in this way. On the one hand, the authorities say alcohol is partly to blame when football crowds start fighting. On the other hand, some of the most famous soccer teams are paid to wear the logos of drinks companies on their shirts.

Of course, saying this does not excuse the violence. But

Sponsorship of sport is now big business.

drink companies know which sports are watched mainly by their target audience, such as young men. Sponsorship is about influencing how they spend their money. It gets them to associate alcohol with being manly and successful.

Pressure from friends

You may have heard the term "peer pressure." It means that most of us want to fit in with the behavior of people we identify with. They are like us – we want to be like them. Few people enjoy being the odd one out.

When you are young, the pressure from friends can be strong. You may feel that, in order to belong to a particular group, you have to talk like them, dress like them, and listen to the same music. If part of their shared activity is smoking or having too much to drink on Saturday night, you may feel you have to do the same. Perhaps they will call you "chicken" if you do not buy and share cigarettes, or "mean" if you do not buy as much to drink as them.

> ❝ *A man may take to drink because he feels himself to be a failure and then fail all the more completely because he drinks.* **Author George Orwell.** ❞

Sometimes you may prefer to have different friends, but you cannot seem to find any. If you live in the country, a bar or club may be the only place to meet. In the city there may be other places to go, but smoking and drinking still seem to be part of a night out.

Luckily, most young people do not smoke. If they drink, it's only reasonable amounts. It is not weak or "chicken" to think for yourself. Friends who force you to do things that you know will harm you, are not the best friends to have. For ideas about how to deal with peer pressure, read the last chapter of this book.

"I can handle it"

You could call one of the pressures to take drugs the "pressure of ignorance." Some people do not realize there is any pressure. Others recognize it but they just do not want to think about the problems their habits may bring.

It is tempting to think, especially when you are young, that "I can handle it" or "It will never happen to me." But all the

Pressure to drink is strong at parties.

thousands of people who die from smoking every year probably thought the same thing. Nearly all of them started smoking before they were 20 years old, thinking they could easily give it up when they wanted to. They were wrong.

Once you get addicted to nicotine, it creates its own pressure. You crave for the next cigarette. You panic if you run out. You walk the cold streets at night, looking for a late-opening store or cigarette machine – like other smokers.

Drinking can also get an early hold on you. You may feel pressured into proving you can "hold your liquor." But one of the effects of alcohol is to take away your judgment of when to stop. Even a single heavy drinking session could lead to something you will regret. You would not be the first girl to get pregnant when drunk; you would not be the first person to jump behind a steering wheel and maim or kill someone as a drunken driver. If you want to enjoy alcohol, and not have it wreck your life, you have to use it wisely.

The manufacturers of cigarettes and alcoholic drinks are not eager to point out the dangers. If you are willing to buy, they are willing to sell. But trends change. There is now a lot of public pressure for public places such as movie theaters, restaurants, trains, and aircraft to be free of smoke. Most young men – and women – prefer not to develop a "beer belly."

When I started work I used to go to the bar during the lunch hour. Pretty soon I couldn't do any work in the afternoons. When they fired me, I had nothing else to do except drink all day. I just wish I'd never started. Lynn, aged 21.

ILLEGAL DRUGS

❝ *You're not dealing with emotions all the time you're addicted...* ❞

WARNING

:RE ARE PLAIN-CLOTHES POLICE OFFICERS O|
IIS THEATRE BY ARRANGEMENT WITH THE MANA

PERSON SUSPECTED OF USING OR SELLING D
LICIT SUBSTANCES OF ANY KIND WILL BE E
ID/OR HANDED OVER TO THE OFFICERS MENTI

DRUGS? DON'T

Most people who have tried illegal drugs have done it only once or very occasionally. They have probably tried marijuana or amphetamines, and usually it is at a party, where the drugs are given to them by friends. The main reason they try is a sense of experiment. They want to see what all the fuss is about. Once their curiosity is satisfied, they are unlikely to try the drug again.

But some do go on to take drugs regularly. And some become addicted.

Peer pressure

Some of the pressure to take illegal drugs is the same as for cigarettes and alcohol (page 31). Once again, a lot depends

Young drug users undergo tests in a rehabilitation unit.

on the people around you. If your friends take drugs, you may find it hard to be the odd one out. This is known as peer pressure.

If we believe every sensational newspaper report about young people and drugs, we might conclude that almost everyone is doing it. Of course this is not true. Most young people *do not* take illegal drugs. Newspapers and "news" features *do* exaggerate.

Being different – together

On the one hand, the fact that some drugs are illegal can make them seem more exciting. To some young people, smoking cigarettes or drinking alcohol is too commonplace. They are drawn instead to the idea of "forbidden fruit" as an act of rebellion, and they actively seek out friends who feel the same. Taking drugs may be the only thing these "friends" have in common. Without the drugs the friendship would end quickly.

However, people using drugs develop an attitude toward this negative behavior. They turn it into a positive thing, and ensure themselves a ready supply of drugs from several sources. It makes them feel part of a special group that takes particular risks. They have their own slang words, and rather secretive ways. It is a "club."

They may also see drug taking as a way of frightening or shocking other people, especially adults. Years ago, when glue sniffing was first reported in the press, some young people thought it was a way to get noticed. Perhaps someone would come and photograph them. Perhaps they

Drugs and money change hands in a street deal.

would be famous, or infamous, if only for a day.

> 66 *I always used to imagine a drug pusher as an evil looking person outside the school gates, but it was this rich girl from private school who gave me my first dope.* **Young male drug user.** 99

Fashionable?

Illegal drugs tend to go in and out of fashion. Sometimes a craze for taking a particular drug will sweep through a neighborhood or city, just as other crazes do.

Drugs are linked with particular styles. In the 1960s many hippies smoked marijuana and some tried LSD. Their music and song lyrics reflected the sensations they experienced. In the late 1970s glue sniffing had its day, linked with heavy rock and punk styles. In the 1980s "acid house" was in the headlines. This time the music was linked to amphetamine use and large-scale parties lasting all weekend.

This air of style and fashion disguises the real dangers. Many rock stars who have been associated with particular drugs now speak out against them. Other members of their bands and other pop heroes have "burned out" on drugs, and several have died. Most young people are wise enough to enjoy the style and the music without relying on and falling victim to the drugs.

❝❝ *In all my drinking and drugging days I never was facing anything ... In terms of maturity I'm really miles behind most people ... you're not dealing with emotions all the time you're addicted.* Eric Clapton, guitarist: survivor of heroin and alcoholism. ❞❞

Having problems

Aside from the special cultural pressures that act mainly on young people, there are personal and social pressures too. Being poor or unemployed, living in a run-down place, feeling life holds no opportunities – all of these can make you look for a short cut to feeling good. No one enjoys being depressed and frustrated.

Most people still find ways of being happy. They find support in friends and family. They find a passionate interest in sports or in music, or in making plans for the future.

Most people enjoy themselves without drugs.

But some people with problems start using drugs to numb their pain. Or else they use drugs to get a temporary feeling of elation – a "high." The effect does not last long.

When it passes, the problems are still there. In fact, taking drugs has made matters worse for them. Now they have less money, they can lose their job or get into trouble with the law. And if they continue, the effects on their health will start to show.

Many problems have nothing to do with being poor. Sometimes they are about being in a racial or cultural minority, or about feeling that you have been excluded or discriminated against. Sometimes they have to do with feeling unloved or neglected. It can happen to wealthy children at expensive schools, as well as to children living in great poverty. Many people feel this way in adolescence, when they are changing and growing so fast. They feel that no one cares or understands what they are going through. This is rarely true. Parents went through it, too.

Availability

If drugs are easily available, there is usually more pressure to use them. That is why the authorities try to keep illegal drugs out of circulation. They clamp down hard on people supplying drugs or allowing their premises to be used for any type of drug abuse. Similarly, the ruling bodies in sports conduct routine checks to stop drugs from getting a hold. If some people get away with it then other sports people will feel the pressure to use them in order to compete and win.

Getting hooked

Some people start using drugs as a "crutch," to help them get along. But many drugs have the power to enter every cell in the body. They actually become a part of you, changing your behavior and your personality. Both your mind and body can be addicted (psychological and physical addiction). It's wrong to think that psychological addiction is less serious and that it is "all in the mind." In fact, psychological addiction can be the hardest to cure.

Being addicted, or hooked, is the biggest pressure of all. It is a form of slavery. Take the heroin addict. Because the body builds up a tolerance to heroin, bigger and bigger doses are needed to get the same effect. Heroin addicts

Young people may feel no one cares or understands.

become obsessed with getting more heroin. Their whole life starts to revolve around the rituals of drug taking, and they become very boring to non-drug users. Before long, heroin becomes so important to them that they forget to eat. They are ready to lie and steal from friends or family or turn to prostitution – anything to get enough money for another "fix." One of the most obvious ways is to sell heroin to other people. In this way the spiral of pressure takes another twist.

The drugs scene

Once illegal drug taking spreads, whole communities can get "hooked." This has happened in several cities with cocaine and crack.

Dealing in illegal drugs is a criminal activity. Those at the top of the supply pyramid – the drug barons – put pressure on those in the middle. They in turn put pressure on the street dealers, or "pushers," who then put pressure on the users. The people at the top surround themselves with protection. Those low in the pyramid take more risks.

❝ *It was her boyfriend who first gave her heroin. She was 16. He got her addicted and kept her supplied. She died four years ago.* **Mother of heroin victim.** ❞

One of the dangers with using any kind of illegal drug is

Heroin is a highly addictive and dangerous drug.

that you come in contact with "the drug scene," even if only the very edge of it. It is not like buying goods at a store, where there is a regular supply and you can depend on the quality. How will you know if the drug is pure? It could be cut or mixed with something poisonous or harmful. How will you know its strength? And if your usual drug is not available, will the dealer persuade you to take something different?

❝ My regular supplier was arrested. Suddenly I had to find a new source. I was like a lost child. New York business executive aged 28. **❞**

THE ROLE OF GOVERNMENT

❝*No one can calculate how much it all costs.*❞

A first duty of any government is to protect its people from harm. But good government is also about protecting its people's freedom. Sometimes this means the freedom to make mistakes. None of us likes being dictated to. So where should governments draw the line?

The law

In the case of strong medical drugs, most countries have strict rules about who can prescribe them and who can dispense them. You have to be qualified in either case. Problems do arise when new medical drugs are tested. Someone has to be the first to try them. Sometimes the side-effects are slow to appear. If there is no other hope of a cure, should an untested drug be given? Who is responsible when things go wrong? These are questions that have to be answered by the government and by the courts.

The use of alcohol and tobacco has such a long history that governments have brought in various laws over the years to control these drugs. In the case of alcohol, they make rules about how strong it is, and what size measures it can be sold in, and the age of the buyers. They restrict the hours of sale, and forbid sales on "unlicensed" premises. They also set a limit to stop people from driving with excess alcohol in their blood. And they keep up the price with the help of taxes.

The clampdown on tobacco has come more recently. Evidence about the health risks – both for smokers and non-

Smoking marijuana causes hallucination and false perception.

smokers – has forced governments to act. Many now restrict advertising, and ban people from smoking in public places or on public transportation. They make cigarette packages carry a health warning. And, again, they levy taxes on cigarettes and tobacco.

Certain other drugs have been made illegal altogether. Customs officials have the task of keeping them out of the country. Anyone selling or making them can expect to receive a heavy fine or a prison sentence. Simply possessing or using them may also be illegal. Because these drugs are outside the law, there is no control over how strong they are or whether they have been "bulked out" with cheaper substances.

Public pressure

Over the years, many of these laws have been the subject of fierce argument. A hundred years ago the brewers and distillers of alcohol fought against laws that restricted their trade, just as the tobacco companies today argue against controls on smoking. Usually, their main concern is their profits, not the public's health. On the other hand, doctors and other health professionals lobby governments to take stronger action. They see the misery that results from drug abuse, and they are particularly concerned about young people.

Laws have often come about as a result of public pressure and lobbying by pressure groups. Today, some groups

Cramped or high-rise accommodation can cause stress.

argue that marijuana should be taken off the list of illegal drugs, because it is no more harmful than alcohol or tobacco. The use of marijuana is now accepted in one or two countries, while in many parts of the world the controls on smoking tobacco and the laws against hard drugs are getting tougher.

Governments under pressure

Because drug taking is so widespread, governments are under pressure to find a solution. Drugs do not only affect those who use them. They have a big impact on the health of society as a whole.

Some people believe that drug taking is a symptom of deeper problems. They say it will get worse until the root causes are dealt with. They want governments to tackle poverty and homelessness, both in rural areas and in the inner cities. This would help give people some hope and self-esteem.

Another form of help would be efforts to lessen stress. For example, public transportation could be faster, cleaner and cheaper. Cutting down on pollution would clean up the environment. More funds for schools, flexible working hours, better child care, and many more local facilities for young people would all help. So would better forms of support for people at times of personal crisis. Then they might not need the "crutch" of drugs.

All this would cost money. But then, so do detoxification programs, drug education, health care for drug victims, fires, accidents, police work on drug problems, and keeping

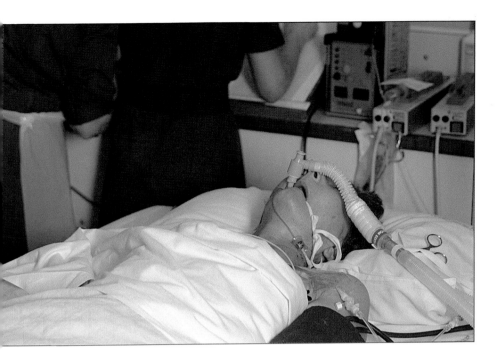

The price of addiction: intensive care.

people in prison. No one can calculate how much it all costs, especially if you include all the millions of working days lost through drug-related illness.

Responsibility

Governments do not deserve all the responsibility. We all have to shoulder our own share, as members of society. But it is clear that governments can help. They have had success in persuading people not to drink and drive. They have helped to wean people away from smoking. They are beginning to tackle illegal drugs through international cooperation and more positive action against the producers and distributors, as well as the users.

Cigarettes cause the smoker to feel temporarily more relaxed.

Alternatives

Imagine what we could do with all the money that is being spent on drugs. Imagine the sports and leisure facilities we could build, the parks and the new homes. Imagine the vacations or the fun you could have on the money that the average smoker spends every year on cigarettes. These are the kinds of choices we have, both as individuals and as a community. Governments can help to set the scene, but we all have decisions to make.

RESISTING THE PRESSURE

"I want to get rid of my problems, not add another one."

What kind of pressures are put on *you*? And what ideas do you have for resisting?

When thinking about how to resist pressure, it is a good idea to imagine particular circumstances and practice how you would deal with them. Some situations where drugs are used can be avoided. You can stay away from the corner of the park where kids sniff glue. You can steer clear of the drinking crowd on their night out. But sometimes situations crop up anyway.

"No thanks, because ..."

You meet new friends and they pass around cigarettes. "Go on, it's cool. Everyone does it." Not true. Most adults do not smoke. Most young people do not smoke. Have an answer ready. "Thanks, but no thanks, I can't stand the smell," or "It makes me breathless and I need to stay in shape," or "No, each cigarette takes five minutes off a life."

You are at a disco. Someone has a few drops of drug on little squares of blotting paper. "Go on, you'll last the night. You'll have a good time." Maybe, but then again it might make you sick. And how about tomorrow? Think about the let-down. Make a joke. "No thanks, I've got natural speed. I don't need that stuff to keep me going."

You are in trouble, and telling your problems to an older friend. He offers you powder to snort. "Go on, it'll kill the pain. You won't get addicted." How does he know? Some people get addicted more easily than others. All addicts

Pressure to roll cigarettes or joints can come from friends.

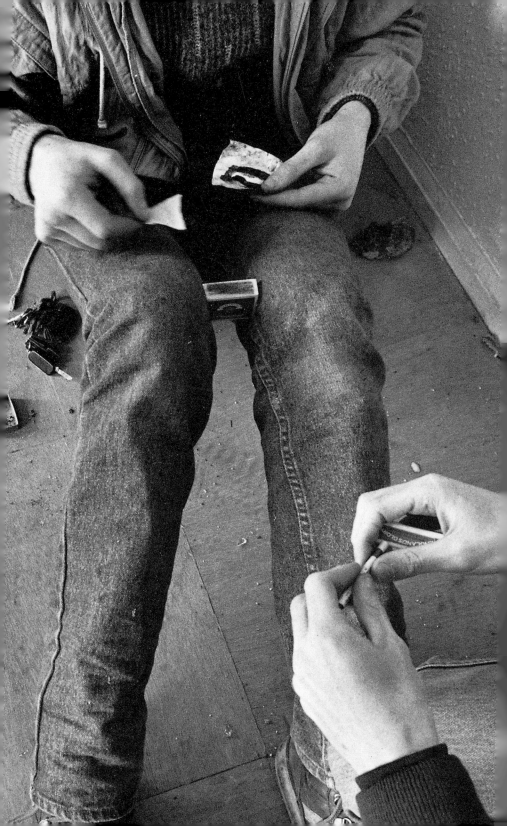

once thought they could handle it.

"You only get addicted if you inject." Not true. Why are they trying to persuade you, anyway? What do they want in return? Be firm in your reply. "No thanks, I need to think straight. I want to get rid of my problems, not add another one." Or "I don't want to run away from my problems. I'd rather face them."

You are at a party. People are passing around something that looks like a skinny cigarette. "Go on, this stuff is high quality." What guarantees do you have? Does anyone really know? You might try: "No thanks, that stuff burns my throat," or "It makes me sick," or "No, I get too paranoid on that."

Exams are coming up. You are out with friends, but feeling anxious. Someone fills your glass with liquor. "Go on, it'll drown your sorrows." Remember, most sorrows can swim! Even if you drink it, they may well fill your glass again. Think about how you could feel in the morning. Hand the glass back. Say something like "No thanks, I'm in training," or "No, I want to stay sober," or "I can't afford a hangover."

Think hard

Ask yourself how many smokers you know who have survived lung cancer. Chances are: none. Less than one out of every ten lung cancer victims survives for more than five years. Think about rock and sports stars who have died.

Think about the effects on your body if you take not just one drug but several, as many people do. For example, alcohol is a depressant, but amphetamines speed you up.

Singer Janis Joplin, whose death was linked with drugs.

Think of the effects of such a mixture, and how your body will be struggling to get back into balance.

Think about the people at the top of the pyramid ... not just the illegal drugs barons, but the cigarette and drink manufacturers too. Think about the money they make.

Think hard about advertisements. What are they really saying? How are they trying to influence you?

Think hard about yourself, and what you want from life. Is a quick "fix" or a short-lived "high" really what you need? Do you want to be chained to a drug habit, wasting your hard-earned cash on it 20 years from now?

Finally, think about different ways to have fun. Think about what's best for you.

FACTFILE

Where pressures come from

Many aspects of modern life carry the temptations and pressures to use drugs, both legally and illegally. Some of them are obvious, some are more hidden. Here are some examples.

Parents and relatives

Older family members may use different drugs to those used by young people today. In some regions more older adults tend to smoke, compared to youger adults, since smoking was more common-place a generation or two ago. Such older people have often lost sight of the fact that they are taking a "drug" at all, and perhaps even abusing it, because it has been a part of their lifestyle for so long.

Peer pressure

This comes from friends and colleagues. Taking drugs sometimes seems to have the appeal of being in a "secret club," or it may be interpreted as an act of rebellion against authority. However, "friendship" based on drug taking is unlikely to be deep and meaningful.

Examples set by the famous

Well-known sports people, music and movie stars, comedians and others in the public eye may disclose that they use drugs. Or their "secret" may be revealed by investigations. However, such revelations usually mark the end of their career.

Advertisements

We are surrounded by adverts, in many forms and guises. Obvious examples are roadside poster hoardings and commercial breaks on television. Less obvious are sponsorship deals in sports or the arts. An athlete, for example, may be seen relaxing with a particular drink, or a rock star may smoke a particular brand of cigarette on stage.

Social pressure, stress and worry

The pressures of modern life may seem to make drugs an answer or a solution. This can range from drinking a morning cup of coffee, as a "pick-me-up," to the busy executive who takes amphetamines with the aim of working through the night to meet a deadline. But drugs only mask the pressure temporarily. Relying on them adds another problem to a load which is already too heavy for the individual to carry.

Disease and illness

Many people, when they become ill, think at once that there must be a pill or medicine that will cure them. In many situations it would be more appropriate to consider a change in lifestyle, or better eating habits, or not working so hard, or changing the circle of friends.

Emotional problems are often better dealt with by bringing them into the open and talking them through, rather than suppressing them and bottling them up with drugs.

Doctors are also subjected to many pressures, in their decision about which drug to dispense. They may be affected by adverts in the medical publications, drug company "gifts" in various disguises, and invitations to medical conferences in exotic locations.

DRUG PROFILE

Common names
Alcohol Contained in beers, lagers, ales, wines, sherries and spirits. Depresses the nervous system and causes drowsiness, blurred vision, clumsiness, unsteadiness, slurred speech, poor memory, headache, nausea, vomiting, collapse and even coma or death.

Nicotine Found in tobacco in its various forms, such as cigarettes, cigars, pipe tobacco, tobacco chews, snuff. Acts as a stimulant and causes increased heart rate and blood pressure. However, other constituents of tobacco smoke, such as tars and carbon monoxide, can cause health problems such as heart diseases and cancers, as well as harming the developing baby when a pregnant woman smokes.

Caffeine Found in drinks such as coffees, teas, chocolate and some soft drinks. Acts as a stimulant on the nervous system and can cause increased heart rate, heart flutters, raised blood pressure, trembling, diarrhea, indigestion and sleeplessness.

Illegal drugs Include heroin, made from opium poppies; cocaine and crack, made from coca plants; marijuana, made from cannabis plants; and various laboratory-made drugs such as LSD ("acid"), "ecstasy," PCP ("angel dust"), and forms of amphetamines ("speed"). Since they are illegal, there is no control or guarantee of their purity and dosage.

Abuse of legal products Solvent-based products are not illegal as such, but they have been misused, usually by inhalation. They include glues, paints and paint-strippers, aerosols such as hair lacquer, and cooking-gas containers.

SOURCES OF HELP

Here are addresses and telephone numbers of organizations that may be able to provide further information on LSD, its effects, health risks and legal status.

National Hotlines
National Institute on Drug Abuse Treatment Referral
1 (800) 622-HELP
Weekdays: 9:00 am – 3:00 am, weekends: 12 noon – 3:00 am.
Counselors are on hand if you need someone to talk to; also call for referrals in your area or if you have a question about drugs, drug treatment, health or legal problems.

New York State Division of Substance Abuse
1 (800) 522-5353
Over-the-telephone crisis intervention by experienced counselors. Also call for referrals or advice.

National Association of State Boards of Education
P.O. Box 1176
Alexandria, VA 22313
(703) 684-4000
Booklet available.

National Clearinghouse for Drug Abuse Information
P.O. Box 2305
Rockville, MD 20850
Provides information on a variety of drugs.

National Self Help Clearinghouse
33 West 42nd Street
New York, N.Y. 10036
(212) 840-1259
Provides information on self-help rehabilitation organizations and clearinghouses throughout the country.

Alcohol and Drug Problems Association of North America
444 N. Capitol Street
Suite 181
Washington, D.C. 20001
(202) 737-4340
Answers inquiries, makes referrals.

Alcohol, Drug Abuse and Mental Health Administration
Public Health Service
Department of Health and Human Services
Parklawn Building
Room 12C-15
5600 Fishers Lane
Rockville, MD 20857
(301) 443-3783
Handles inquiries, fills requests for publications.

American Civil Council for Drug Education
6193 Executive Boulevard
Rockville, MD 20852
(301) 984-5700
Answers inquiries, conducts workshops, distributes publications and makes referrals.

Drug and Alcohol Council
396 Alexander Street
Rochester, N.Y. 14407
(716) 244-3190
Answers inquiries, provides advisory services, distributes publications and makes referrals.

National Network of Youth Advisory Boards
P.O. Box 402036
Ocean View Beach
Miami, FL 33140
(305) 532-2607
Answers inquiries, provides advisory and consulting services.

WHAT THE WORDS MEAN

addictive causing physical or psychological need for the drug in order for the user to stay "normal" and stave off the physical and mental effects of withdrawal

alcoholism being dependent on the drug alcohol, which must be taken regularly to stave off withdrawal symptoms (popularly known as "DTs")

antibiotic a drug that fights against infection, usually caused by bacteria; many antibiotics are not effective against viral infections

drug any chemical or other substance that changes the body's working (including the way the person's mind works, behavior, etc.)

drug abuse non-medical drug use with harmful effects, on the abuser and possibly on others

drug baron an everyday term for a person in charge of a large drug manufacturing and/or distributing organization, who is usually exceedingly rich due to the illegal but high profits of this business

drug misuse using drugs in a way which people in general would see as not sensible, or not acceptable, and possibly harmful

hard drug a confusing term usually used to describe a drug which has powerful effects and which can be addictive; it tends to refer to illegal drugs. Heroin certainly comes into this group. But some may argue that so does alcohol, yet it is regarded in many regions as far less dangerous than heroin and a drug to be used "socially"

"high" the temporary feelings of relaxation, pleasure or elation caused by taking a certain type of drug; it is often followed by a "low" of depression and tiredness as the drug's effects wear off

logo a small graphic device, such as a geometric shape or an illustration or some specially-shaped writing, that is the symbol of a company or brand name; it is often used in advertising

medicinal drug a drug used by doctors and other health professionals with the aim of speeding healing, curing disease, easing symptoms or preventing illness

peer pressure the feeling that we should "fit in" with our friends, colleagues and contemporaries, and do what they do

sponsorship when an organization, usually a commercial company, puts up money to fund an event (such as a sports match or art exhibition), in return for publicity in the form of posters, logos, advertisements and perhaps its name incorporated into the title of the event

INDEX

Photographic Credits:
Cover and pages 14, 18, 19, 52 and 53: Roger Vlitos; pages 4, 7, 21, 31, 40, 49 and 57: Topham Picture Library; pages 9, 33, 42 and 43: Rex Features; page 10: Stuart Franklin/Magnum Photos; page 12: Niblock-Stuart; pages 16, 28 and 38: Marie-Helene Bradley; pages 24 and 27: Robert Harding Library; page 35: Sparham/Network Photographers; pages 36 and 55: Peter Marlow/Magnum Photos; page 45: Frank Spooner Agency; page 47: Magnum Photos; page 51: Chris Steele-Perkins/Magnum Photos.